BOTTLED HISTORY

ENVISAGE BOOKS

BOTTLED HISTORY

Feints, fellows and photographs

Vestiges of a disappearing era
in Scottish malt whisky distilleries

Ian Macilwain
Foreword by Jim McEwan

Design by Eddie Ephraums
Envisage Books

To Maggie

For her unwavering support and love,
without which I would never have
persisted to the end.

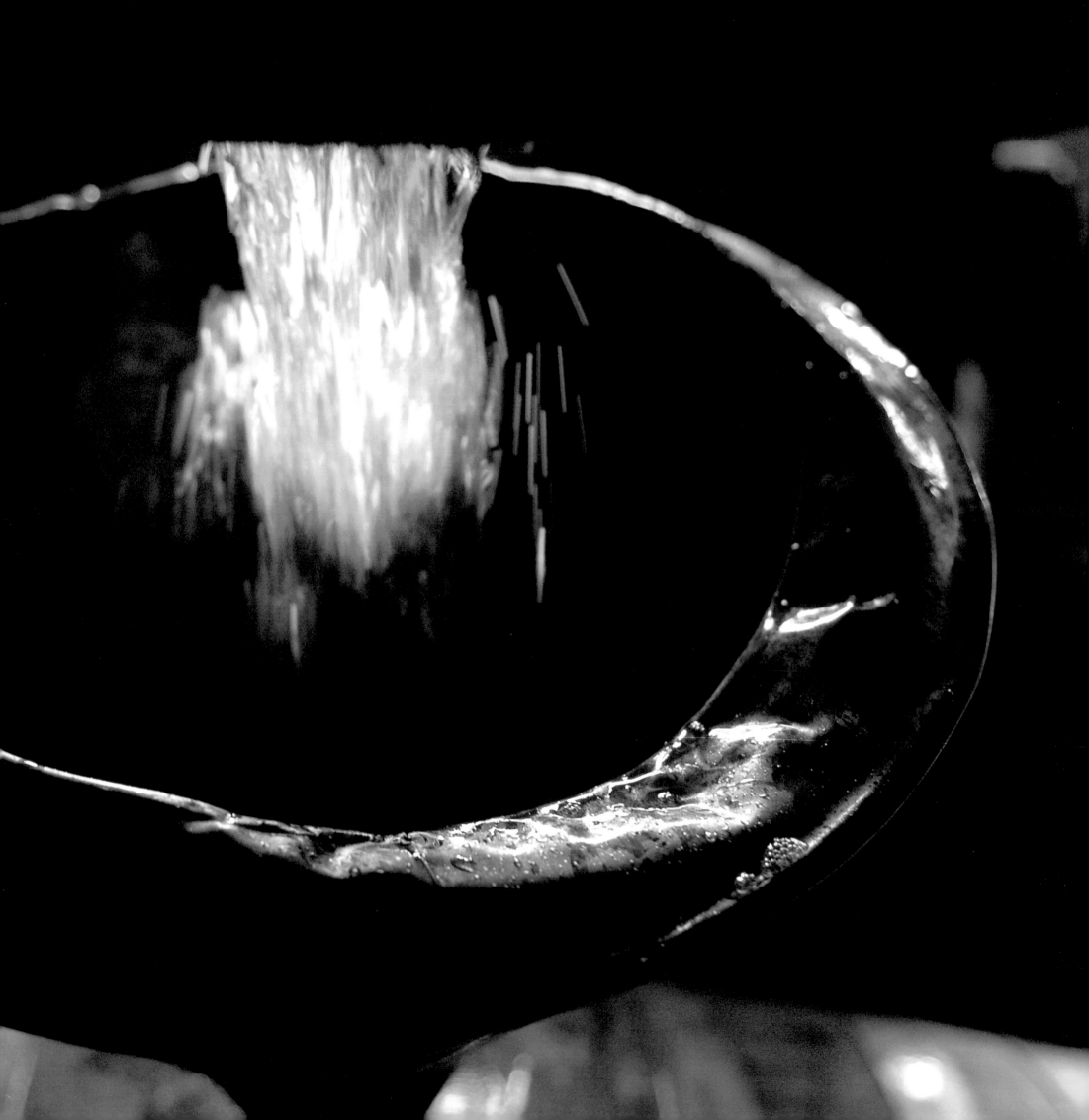

CONTENTS

Foreword

Jim McEwan

Introduction

Ian Macilwain
Technical terms – Dictionary

Vestiges

Raw materials – Steeping – Germination – Kilning – Milling – Mashing
Fermentation – First distillation – Second distillation – Maturation

Thumbnails

Acknowledgments

Foreword

Jim McEwan

I first met Ian five years ago, when he stopped by the distillery and asked if it would be possible to take some photographs there. We had a long chat over a dram or two about the book he was planning to write. He showed me some of the photographs he had already taken and, for me, having been in the business for more than 40 years at that time, it was like taking a walk down memory lane. But it is when the pictures are matched to the quotes that the book really starts to come alive, and it's easy to imagine the characters who made such beautiful single malts – the likes of which we will never taste again.

Ian's love for the 'blood of Scotland' burned brightly as he described the story of his journey round the distilleries. It brought to mind a similar journey made by Alfred Barnard during the late 1880s, whereby he recorded an amazing production record of more than 129 distilleries. This book possibly forms the last record of distilling equipment from a time when the art of distillation was truly a unique skill, honed over hundreds of years and passed down from generation to generation. Today, sadly, it is computers and consultants who are the new 'Kings of the Stills'. However, Ian's book will forever give us the opportunity and pleasure to return to what were truly the golden years of single malt production – when steam provided the power and people the passion.

Introduction

Ian Macilwain

I can think of no other product on the market that contains within it a kind of time capsule. Scottish malt whisky is a handcrafted liquid made at a specific place and time. Its era of manufacture is frozen within it at the point when it enters the bottle. This means that, for upwards of £50 at current rates, you can acquire a product made at a time prior to automation and multinational ownership, and which will reflect in its character the production methods of that age. One could say that it is indeed a 'bottled history'!

I first tasted single malt whisky in 1969 at the age of 20. My cousin, who is one of the interviewees in this book, was at that time employed as the excise officer at Auchentoshan distillery in Dumbarton. Every year at Christmas he received his allocation from the company of several gallons of matured, cask-strength spirit. Generously, he dispatched a sizable part of this to deserving relatives like my father! On an annual basis, for several years, a plastic squash bottle full of Auchentoshan would duly arrive. We would sample this precious spirit with due reverence.

When I moved to Aberdeen to undergo a medical training it did not take long to realise that I was on the edge of the largest concentration of malt whisky distilleries in the world. On one occasion I went to the village of Aberlour in Speyside as part of a social medicine project, only to learn that there were 13 distilleries within the boundaries of this small general medical practice.

I started to read about whisky production and visited those distilleries close at hand, such as Glengarioch at Old Meldrum and Glendronach at Forgue. I remember my first sight of the mystery of floor maltings and the overwhelming, intoxicating smell of distilling spirit from the still house. It still has an effect on me now, some 35 years later.

About ten years ago I acquired, quite accidentally, a reprinted version of Alfred Barnard's iconic book, The Whisky Distilleries of the United Kingdom, first published in 1886. The stories it contained – and particularly his way of telling them – instantly captivated me. The beginnings of an idea began to formulate. I thought it would be a fascinating exercise to attempt to revisit all the distilleries he had described, and photograph them in their current state. Around the turn of the millennium I began to do this, albeit in a rather unstructured way. At this time I was acutely aware of my forthcoming retirement from health service psychiatry, due in 2004. Photography had been a lifelong interest of mine, initially stimulated by my father's darkroom, which he maintained in the attic of our house. I began to take photographic commissions, starting initially with weddings and then followed by an industrial project which came my way by accident through a connection with Aberdeen Industrial Doctors. It just happened that this company provided medical services to Inverhouse Distillers, and I was provided with an introduction by Dr Ewan Thomson and an invitation to visit the small Knockdhu distillery, where I met Malcolm Waring, the manager. The rest, as they say, is history.

It rapidly became apparent to me that, rather like an archeological exploration, most distilleries (particularly the smaller, older ones) contained traces of former practices. Sometimes whole sections had been walled off and forgotten. They were just waiting for me to photograph them.

I became fascinated by the idea of collecting stories from retired employees of the distilling industry, who would be able to recall the working climate of the era before automation. The fact that Malcolm had arranged my first interviews with three particularly engaging men undoubtedly gave me the encouragement to continue.

Any person knowledgeable about malt whisky may wonder why many famous distilleries are missing from this project. In fact, I visited almost all the distilleries in Scotland, but many have created such an immaculate environment that I was unable to find the dark corners and disused equipment which constitute the heart of this project. Distilleries such as Glengoyne, Auchentoshan, Glenmorangie, Glenrothes and Glenfiddich are beautiful examples of immaculate current practice. I in no way mean to imply anything negative by their absence from this project. On the contrary, I celebrate the way in which such companies have raised the profile of malt whisky internationally.

It will also be noted that there are significantly more pictures from Bruichladdich and Springbank than from anywhere else. This is purely because I have spent long periods of time in both distilleries and have had much greater opportunity to seek out interesting pictures than in relatively brief chaperoned visits.

Last year I underwent a four-day academy training programme run by Jim McEwan at Bruichladdich distillery in Islay. I am particularly delighted that he agreed to write the foreword to this book. No one has been a better ambassador for this industry than he. His tireless energy has to be witnessed to be believed.

I'm also delighted that Eddie Ephraums showed such willingness and enthusiasm to become involved in the publication. Through his work, particularly in the field of landscape photography and self-publishing, he has become a well-known name in the field.

We wanted the layout of the book to be as simple and aesthetically satisfying as possible. For this reason there is nothing to detract from the photographs and their accompanying text. However, the rear of the book contains information regarding both photographs and interviewees. It is hoped that the organising system is sufficiently self-explanatory to allow a more complete integration of the various components.

I'll be delighted to receive any feedback, which will ultimately be incorporated in the production of a soft cover version.

Technical terms

Draff – the waste husks of the barley after mashing, used for cattle feed

Dunnage – an earth floor warehouse

Excise men – the government tax officer, was resident until 1975

Hog's Heads – large casks

Making the barley – germinating the barley before kilning it

Mashing – a porridge of crushed malted barley with hot water

Mash tun – the large vessel usually with a brass lid in which the mash is made

Malt floor – a football pitch size floor covered with soaked barley to allow germination

Pot ale – the liquid waste from the distilling process

Saladin Boxes – a semi automated way of turning the germinating barley using mechanical means

Set wire – a wire used to measure the shape of a still by making a template

Strip the kiln – to empty the kiln when the barley has been dried out by the hot air

Shooks – bundles of dismantled barrel staves

Staves – wooden pieces which fit together to make the barrel

Steep – the concrete or metal trough for soaking the barley before germination

Swan neck – the top part of the distillation still

Switchers – the revolving arm on a washback to stop froth from the fermentation from running over the lip

Racked warehouse – new type with concrete floor with many layers of casks in a rack

Turn the floor over – use a spade to turn over the thick barley layer

Tun room – the room containing six or more huge fermenting containers made of wood or steel. (washbacks)

Turner – the stirring apparatus in a mash tun

Washback – the huge fermenting vessel (see tun room)

Worms – the long revolving spiral used to transport malted barley or coal

Wort – the sugary gruel from the drained mashtun which is sent to the washback for fermentation

Dictionary

Ain – own

Barrow – wheelbarrow

Bob – old shilling (pre decimal)

Burn – stream

Bookie – betting shop

Cowped – tipped

Chitty – betting slip

Dram – a measure of clear spirit from the stills given to the workforce several times per day and also as a reward for dirty or unpleasant tasks

Dross – bits of coal

Doon – down

Fit why? – why is that?

Fae – from

Gaein – giving

Himsel – himself

Hame – home

Jist – just

Ken – you know

Loon – boy/youth

Nah – no

New start – new boy

Oot – out

Pit – put

Park – field

Peterheid – Peterhead

Pit awa fae – sacked

Piece – snack

Pow – prisoner of war

Pit ye off – put you off

Quines – girls/young women

Roond – round

Reviver – dram

Sarkin – roof boards under the slates

Served their time – completed an apprenticeship

Stotterin – staggering about

Tae – to

Tatties – potatoes

Wis doin onything wrang – wasn't doing anything wrong

Ye ken – you know

"It didn't really matter if the peat wasn't completely dry
as all they wanted was the smoke."

"That's what you did in the summer – cut the peat."

"The first 24 hours was with peat and you had to be careful as peat burns much hotter than anthracite and you could burn the kiln. I had a kiln man with me who had burnt the kiln but it was alright and we could still use it. A lot of people don't believe you that peat burns so hot. It was all local peat. That's what you did in the summer - cut the peat. It didn't really matter if the peat wasn't completely dry as all they wanted was the smoke. You took samples (from the barley) in the morning and then again in the evening and you waited for the moisture content to drop to about four per cent. Then you would strip the kiln."

"Negotiating with the farmers [over barley] was hard.
They always tried to get more, but they got a good price.
There was no animosity with that – but the draff...
when you sold the draff, I've never seen so many moaning
buggers in all my life!"

"On another occasion a group of people was shooting at the nearby Leith Hall estates, and a pheasant landed right beside the man who was sweeping out the burn. He plucked the pheasant and put it to one side, ready to take home, but the hunters' dogs found the pheasant and one of the local gamekeepers saw immediately what had happened and pocketed it for himself. At the end of the hunt the landowner became suspicious that there were not enough pheasants, so he made all the keepers empty their pockets ~ and this plucked pheasant was found inside the clothing of a gamekeeper. He couldn't explain how it came to be plucked. . ."

"We take our water straight from the mains. It's perfectly good for us."

"Everything was driven by one big steam engine, and it's still there. It was my baby. I looked after it and painted it all green and black – it was a beauty. I used to have photographs of it. I took pride it keeping it polished. It powered everything. There were belts just driving the mashing machine, the turner inside the mashing machine, and all the belts for the washbacks and the big switchers. There were belts everywhere, and all the pumps were driven with belts, water pumps, steam pumps for pumping the wort – all out of the same steam engine. You see the fly wheel? In every corner there were spokes and a wheel, and they did all the mashing, milling and grinding – and the kiln there was a turner in there too. That was our sole power. There was very little to break down in these big engines. It was a bit noisy with all the belts going."

"There were mechanical stokers to feed the fires. If you got a bit of coal or a piece of wood it was just a disaster, because it had great long cast iron worms that would jam between the casing. You'd just have to strip it out, take off all the lids - and they were big, heavy lids - and the trouble was they were below the level of the floor. Oh, it was hard work and you'd have to take the floor up as well. It was big square sheets of thick aluminium floor - it was hard going. At that time you could hardly miss a mash - there were ten mashes a week. It was just a disaster if you lost a mash, because they were making the barley and everything would have just had to stop because it was just flowing through. You had to get that thing going. Now they can leave it a week and they don't have to worry so much. There were two boilers to look after - one for the plant and one for the distillery. Everything came in by rail at that time, all the barley and the coal and yeast. There was about 20 tonnes and a boy would just shovel it in. I've seen one lad shift the whole lot before 8 o'clock in the morning."

"I could pass that plant now and tell them what's wrong with it. I actually could save them £20,000 a year just by walking past it. They've got a 14-horsepower motor going 24/7 that they don't need. Even by the smell they've got too much sulphur. And that's just walking past. This is what they used to do years ago - you didn't need to go in if you had the knowledge."

"A manager here - Hardie was his name - he loved the horse. The carter - that was Sandy Lyle at that time - used tae take the horse tae the station and they carted the coal roond here from the station yard. But when the rain came on he put the horse inside and the boys had tae barrow the coal fae the station yard and then they cowped it over the wall in tae the heap, and then he made them whitewash the coal to stop the boys stealing it.

He would go doon an give the horse a piece ye see, and was often found at night cos he had a stable there and the boys went roond and found him lying in atween the horse's feet."

"As a loon I went there at 15. It was quite strange for me as I had no idea of distilling, but I got 15 bob a week. The normal clerk's wage was 10 shillings, but because I had certain circumstances, I had to support my brother as well as myself. I was given 15 shillings and that was to support the two of us. My mother had died so we were left to fend for ourselves basically. There was Glendullan distillery. It was quite a small distillery, which is much bigger now. You covered for everything of course. I think there were only two shifts, mind you, not the normal three shifts. The stillman would do 12 hours for the day shift, and the night shift man would come on and do 12 hours, and that was common. And, of course, when the war came, the only distillery that was kept going in Dufftown was Mortlach. The others closed."

"One of my sadder moments happened at S*** distillery. We had six hog's heads filled in 1923, the year I was born, and in 1983 they were still there and they'd lost the ownership ~ so what did they do? They poured it down the drain! If they'd bottled that ~ I mean it wasn't a great dram, it was about 37 over proof or something ~ they could have genuinely put on the label '60 years old' ~ and what sort of price could you ask for that, regardless of the quality? It wasn't bad; in fact I've still got a drop of it in a bottle ~ it was drinkable. I even suggested that if they were not going to bottle it, why not put it back in the process? To watch it gurgle down the drain was incredible ~ I should've photographed it. If we'd been able, through devious methods, I think we'd have done something with it. I never forgot that. It was my last year at the distillery."

"I was lucky for a while when I retired, as I was able to get Glenfarclas in bulk. I could get a ten-gallon barrel and it cost I think about £100 a gallon, which was very reasonable, and usually I'd spread it out and various people would take a gallon or a bottle. So I've still got a stock of that which I'm working on very carefully. It was ten years old at that time and it was 60 per cent stuff, so it really was a good dram. The difficulty is knowing how long I'm going to live so that I can space it out!"

"When I started there it was quines that pit the casks together. They brought all the 'shooks', they called them, the staves from America, the bourbon casks, took em ower in boats and took them up tae Duffown and the quines put them together. There was 12 quines that did it and they were brilliant, and then when work got short doon in Paisley they started kickin' up a fuss about this, as they (the women) hadnae served their time - they went on strike about the quines. Used tae see them going in in the morning, beautiful painted up, and coming out as black as coal at night. It was really funny tae see them going hame for their supper at night, cos they were just as black as coal, but I tell ye this, when they got pit awa fae [sacked from] the distillery and they started making casks [in Paisley] they were nae nearly as good as the ones the quines made in Dufftown..."

"They used to bring a lot of the barrels over on the Pibroch [the puffer steamer]. The boys would be rolling the barrels along, and you could actually hear the amount left in the barrel if it hadn't been properly emptied by the blenders (say it was Friday afternoon and they were in a hurry). So what you did was, with a bit of chalk, you put a cross on the end of it for future reference and then later on, when all was quiet on the nightshift, they would go and roll the barrel over with something underneath to catch it. Everything was provided for you as they used to use filter papers up in the mash house. You used to filter the stuff just to filter out any impurities like bits of cork. Oh, it was great fun!"

"The head chemist from Invergordon came down and he told me to spray the washbacks with hydrochlorate ~ I think it was about 3:1. And, of course, our production started going down and the head chemists came from Edinburgh and they said to me, 'He's the one ~ he's the one that's in charge.' Well, I wasn't in charge but I suppose I was the head one. He asked what I cleaned the washbacks with. I told him, 3:1 of "chlorus". He said, 'Well, I'll tell you something, it's not only the foe you're killing but the friendly as well ~ just stop it right now!' So we stopped ~ and our production went up. We'd been making it too clean!"

"There was a big steep – you know, where they soaked the barley – and it was metal if I remember right. There was a funeral up at the distillery and the men had to work. Just about the time of the funeral they were all standing up on the edge of this big steep, looking out of the window. Just as the funeral procession passed, a boy fell off the side of the steep and was floundering about in the water. There was all this laughing – we were trying to pull him out and they said this roar went up. I'm sure the folk at the funeral thought it was a cheer."

"There were maltings where you popped the barley at the top of the building and it came down another level to another process and it was steeped and it was spread and it was kilned."

"He'd say, 'Well I think we should maybe give it an extra day.'
'Are you sure?'
'Aye. well we'll just give it another day then.'
He knew himself but he just wanted me to take the decision. He was a cracking lad."

"The malt floors were hard work. When you were in there with the malt shovel, you learned a lot by feel and by moisture. Imagine the fittest you've ever been in your life and then watch this guy turning the malt. It looks easy but the sweat and the back muscles! It's a technique, and it takes years. I was never a maltman but if I'd done it for six months I might have eventually learned this technique. The only way to learn it would be to start at the beginning and work to the end. It was all the old maltmen that did all the physical work."

"What was called stripping the kiln, the amount of dust - they'd no masks or anything. Sometimes you'd go in and you'd hardly see the lad you were working with for dust. Terrible conditions. You got a mask but it didn't work. You see it was the heat came in - well, it was never out really. It went 24 hours. Even when you were stripping the kiln there was still heat coming up. The old way to load it was it came up through a spout and there was a single rail went round. It went underneath this spout, so you ran, filled your bucket and went away round to the other side of the kiln, tipped it over and back round again. Sometimes the boy in the kiln fire - now he used to work Sunday, too - some of them were working about 72 hours a week. They were sometimes getting off at 6 o'clock in the morning and they were on at 6 o'clock at night. Most of the distilleries did it in more or less the same way. They got a lot of chest complaints with the dust. There were no showers at that time, you just went in with a cold pail of water. Of course, a dram always helped!"

"At that time we made four-fifths of our requirement and brought in a 20-tonne lorry load a week. That was using the Saladin boxes. I'd have to say that it was the job I probably enjoyed most at the distillery. We had a head maltman, Charlie Robertson, who'd been across in Canada and really knew his business. He'd been in modern maltings, where you popped the barley at the top of the building, and it came down another level to another process, and it was steeped and it was spread and it was kilned. I picked up a lot from him. So really that was your job - you stripped the kiln when you went into your shift. You went down to the Saladin box, emptied one of the Saladin boxes up into the kiln, then you sterilised and washed out the Saladin box, dropped another batch in and that was kind of your shift finished - that was your daily routine."

"By instinct you learned how to tell when the malt was ready, purely by taking a handful of it between the fingers. And you could just tell by walking on it."

"I didn't like the barns. Too monotonous. You went in in the morning to turn the floor over. You turned it over and you went back in the afternoon and turned it over again. It was really hard work. I was soft - being in the Navy I didn't have to really do any hard work. I was fit enough - but it was still hard to do."

"After kilning the barley we sent samples to the chemist and he would tell you how good your kilning had been, as well as the colour and the alcohol content of the malt. Then you took it up to the store for six months to wait for it to go dormant before it was milled. They maintained that if you milled and stirred it too quickly you wouldn't get the sugar content."

"Back in my lorry driving days I was up at the distillery to take the last load of draff out for the year. There was two with mouth organs and another two dancing the Highland fling in the middle of the malt floor at three in the afternoon! They were well gone. The manager just walked past and 'didn't see'. There was never anything said. Things like that would never happen now."

"In the summer you get a silage pit and you fill it up with draff – lorry loads and lorry loads – cover it over with polythene and keep the air away from it, and it keeps perfectly well for about six or seven months. You can open it up again in the winter time and it's still perfectly good. People were asking me if it had any strength at all. If it's been lying there in that silage pit whatever liquid is in there will have something in it, so no wonder the cattle are fond of it… It's maybe not very strong but they enjoy it anyway."

"There was a 20-tonne batch of malt in there - stripping down the kiln they called it. There was about another 20 tonne of dust in there and I thought, 'What have I let myself in for here?'"

"So Robbie came round with the big copper flagon and the horn, which is just a measure. It was new-made spirit, called clearic. Everybody working at that area lined up by the sink, put on the cold water tap and Robbie filled it up. I went to the back of the queue, as I wasn't sure what they were on! So they poured in the measure with the horn, into the first glass, the first lad cowped it back, in below the cold water tap, cowped it back, gave it a swirl and handed the glass back to the next one. And back it came and back it came to me. I was thinking, 'God I'm nae sure about this,' because I wasn't a drinker and it was strong stuff. I saw they'd all just put it back in a 'wunner' so I thought, here goes . . .' Before I got the water I choked. Robbie asked me something and I was trying to answer him — he says, 'Hold it up again,' and I thought it was an initiation, that I had to do two of these! So he fills it up again, fills up the horn, pours it into the glass and I'm looking at it and he grabs it out of my hand and says, 'Aye it's a poor ship that cannae carry the captain.' He probably had one along with the stillman on the way through and then he had another one along at pour end. What a man he was. He lived into his 90s so it didn't do him any ill!"

"Oh there were characters! We had one chap, I think he was an ex-bobby, very tall and he'd only a few hundred yards to travel from his work to his home. I can always remember him going along the road towards the house and he got slower and slower, it was one of those big bikes with a 28-inch frame, and eventually the bike stopped and he just fell off! I can visualise that yet - he didn't hurt himself, you never do when you've got a drink. That was one of the things that I remember."

"The farmers used to come in with a barrel and get pot ale, which the cattle would sup up in troughs. We used to pump the pot ale up the hill here, and any cattle on the hill at the time would arrive at the exit where the pot ale was coming out and have a good feed of it. They obviously liked it."

"One man was actually retired, but he'd been called back during the war to work, and he was a very excitable character. The old mash tuns were open with a stirrer inside, and were operated by a belt drive. There were three men in the mash tun sweeping it out – they were finished for the day. The boss walked into the mash house and this excitable bloke pulled the first handle that he saw, and it started the mechanism – so here's the rakes going round and the boys inside running away from it! That was a story I got secondhand. Whether there was any truth in it I don't know."

"One man, a bachelor, was a bit odd. He brought in his piece every day to be warmed up on the pipes, like everyone else. His piece was always wrapped up in silver foil and you put your piece on the hot metal pipes and in two or three hours it would be really piping hot. On this particular day somebody took his piece and he couldn't find it anywhere. Then it reappeared in everybody else's piece boxes over the next two or three weeks, becoming more and more mouldy as it went on. Eventually somebody had the courage to throw it out."

"We built the washbacks first out of Finnish pine, not Oregon pine, which everyone seems to think – they couldn't grow enough pine in Oregon. To build the washback you laid a circular base and then you stuck your staves round the side. They had a sort of notch up from the base. Once you had them all on together you put on the whole lot right round, and you had a sort of elongated staple called the dog, which you stuck in to join the two staves together. You went round the whole lot and that was the only thing holding it together. Then you put a strong rope round the bottom end and twisted it really tight with a bar. You had the top all tied together with the dogs, and then you started making hoops. You just made every individual one as no matter how you make them every washback has a slight variation. You dropped your hoop on and there was about eight or ten of you round about with a driver each, and you had to keep in time. And the noise – you could hear it a mile away! Bang. . . bang. . . bang. . . You had to keep in rhythm. We must have done a good job as they've never leaked!"

"I remember I worked with another fella up there who was a heck of a man for the horses – every day with the paper! He was the tun room man, so what he did was to turn on the steam. There was that much steam you couldnae see him. He would be sitting in a wee chair way round the back doing his horses and the manager and the brewer would come down and look in the door and say, 'Ach, Bill's busy!' Then the first lorry driver to come in aboot he would be out with his wee chitty to take to the bookie."

"We used to hae a boy here called Geordie Webster. He was a real character. I remember I came in one Sunday morning. I was drivin' the van, and he said to go in by Brodies and get some bacon – aye, just for himself. When I went back in the afternoon, Geordie had the shovel, gaein it a clean, and broke the eggs 'n' bacon intae the shovel and shoved them intae the fire! One of boys said, 'Smells lovely,' but when ye saw the dross round the edge it pit ye off."

"There is one story that would have come out of this workshop. Old Ally Grant had a son. They went up tae Glenlivet Distillery with the bus tae measure swan necks and get the shape of them. There was nae fancy things at that time so they took a set wire, which is a bit of wire about three feet or less, and took the shapes with the wire. Back at Dufftown the boss said tae them, 'Where's the set wire?' He said, 'Here' — he had straightened them all oot!"

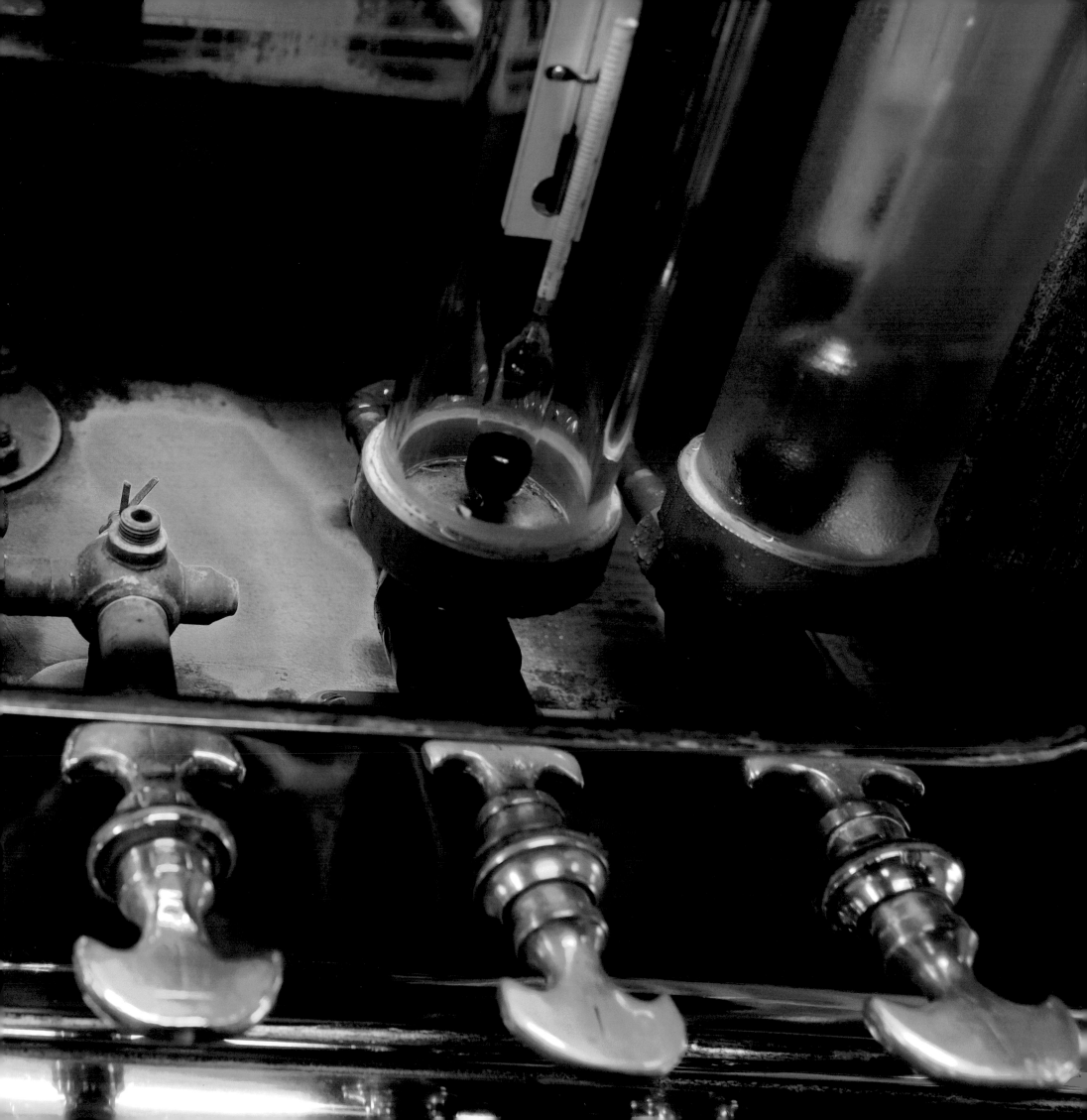

"With about two weeks to go to the end of the season and completion of vital blenders' orders, disaster struck. The paper-thin internal steam coils of the vital old spirit-still burst near a flange. The skilled copper-welder from Edinburgh kept burning through the fragile metal. No hope. Then he and I had a chat and I suggested making a patch slightly larger than the hole which we could slip inside the damaged area of the tubing, hold temporarily in place with a stitch of copper wire and silver braze. He had done none since his tech college course. It was a joint effort. My torch and all the silver solder I had, plus my flux, on the damaged area; a big soft flame from him on the heavy flange nearby to get to the temperature. It worked. Back in an hour or so and the plant back in production soon afterwards. The wonderful thing was still to come. Two weeks later when the season had been completed the coils were sent off to Edinburgh as patterns for new ones. The new ones arrived a few weeks later in sacking, fresh from the Commercial Union Insurance Testing - complete with certificate. But what was this? Other coils, also with a certificate. The old repaired ones had also passed the pressure tests and been certified for limited period use. Wow. I cannot tell you how I felt!"

"They used to try to speed everything up. They would begin the process of distillation before the fermentation was really complete. They used soap containers which would shred soap because it was discovered that it would stop the fermentation in its tracks."

"The queue for the dram was long. I'm making my way along and asked, 'Does the new start take a dram?'

'Yes, join the queue!'

This fellow in front of me just took the glass, which was a fair old measure, and threw it back. I did the same. My god, the steam was coming out of my ears! I felt it going running down my throat. It took the speech from me. I was half way down the street when I got my breath back – it was just the pure clear spirit. If they put too much water in a tipple it used to go cloudy, but the boys would play up so we always got a good clear dram – it was amazing. I stopped at the Mountain Dew on the way down the road and had a nip and a half pint. I can remember I was kind of stottering. It must have been good stuff! Aye, that was my first taste."

"Did people mind that the dram had gone? Oh, some of them did. That's another nail in the coffin, they would say... Everybody had the flu, of course, as it killed every known germ. It was very good as well for washing and cleaning windows [the clear spirit]. We used to clean the windows on the spirit safe with it as well. It seemed to go an awful long way. The fellow that was doing the work managed to get most of it anyway, so not a great deal was used for cleaning!"

"Willie Cowan from Huntly was sorting slates in the warehouse, and he came on a bit o sarkin that was a bit rotten. I was looking out from the cooperage. All I could see was Willie's top half, and he jist ripped it [the sarkin] all oot and was standing on a cask tae get inside a warehoose. There were two locks on the door and ye needed an excise man to get in. Willie had just took a bit of the roof off and one of the excise men walked through the yard for his breakfast. I thought he was gonnae faint. But Willie was quite innocent, didnae think he was doing anything wrong!"

"I've seen bags of tatties going in one door and bottles of whisky going out the other."

"If you take a guy who's 65 years old, retired, take him into the warehouse and say right we're going to give you the run of the warehouse (because it's got everything, it's got concrete floors and earth floors – the lot – dunnage and racked), take as much as you want – every single one would go for the earth floor."

"Like POWs you may rely on whisky to take advantage of any opportunity to 'escape'."

"The auld cooper, Bill Sim, repaired casks and was originally building herring barrels in Peterheid, but then landed at the distillery. He was a genius with the barrels. If there was a cask so much as leaked in the warehouse they would get him tae make a barrel to suit the amount o' whisky that was left in the cask. That was called rackin'. He would look at the cask an say there was about 20, 30 gallon left, and make a cask that size. They were brilliant things made out of staves o' broken casks."

A present-day distiller contemplates his past...

It's all very well to romanticise the past but the reality was hard, dangerous and uncompromising. Technology has freed the distiller from laborious tasks but he must never forget that the product's roots lie in the land, and in the uncontrollable forces of nature, about which it is still necessary to be both humble and reverent.

IFM

On a vernacular society

The barbarians sat amidst the hills of Rome
Sated with almonds and red Tuscan wine
The togas girt about their shaven legs
Their clipped hair plastered down with unguents,
And all remembered home:
                    The reeking hut,
The redwood stockade and the auroch's lowe
Through Odin's land. They had forgot the tongue
Brought through the Alpine pastures, yet all swore
Such rhyme and radiance Latin never knew.
They swore on this in Latin. And one rose,
An elder warrior, he, from Palatine,
And read a paper on the antique speech.
But few could understand, for much of it
Was in that ancient speech. Yet all did cheer.

Some wept, and soon their Latin quantities
Were blurred with wine and memory, till one
Up rose and swore that he would take the road
Back through the Alpine passes, home again,
If they would follow him. At this there fell
A silence of surprise. They looked askance
One on the other, and with upraised hands
Did indicate that in the speaker's skull
Some evil god disported with his brains.
So night came down. Each called his slave and went
Back through the streets of Rome to perfumed baths
And song and dance.
                    They heard the rain that night
Come sheeting from the north, and in their beds
Did turn in wakeful warmth and sleep again.

Lewis Grassic Gibbon

THUMBNAILS

Cover image

Cover image
Warehouse
Balblair distillery, Edderton

It seems fitting to have a distillery from the Inver House group on the cover as they played a large part in galvanising my initial enthusiasm. They also have a number of really interesting but not well known distilleries in their portfolio, of which this is one. A respect for tradition runs through the whole group and a tendency to let things be rather than clean them up, resulted in a lot of photo opportunities for my project.

Pages 4-5
Excise officer's room
Balblair distillery, Edderton

I owe a debt to my cousin, Denzil Chesters, long retired from the position of excise officer to Auchentoshan distillery in Dumbarton. It was through him that, as a teenager, I first tasted long-matured malt whisky, part of the allocation which as a 'company man' in those days he received annually. The excise officers rooms hold a peculiar fascination for me. They have a patina of age augmented by traces of former functions like exercise books and forms still mouldering in the corners. Several of the quotes in the book originate from Denzil.

Foreword

Pages 6-7
Racking
Bruichladdich distillery, Islay

The process of decanting the contents of a cask and transferring it to another is known as racking. Sometimes it needs to be done because evaporation has left too much air space in the cask. At other times a decision has been made to 'finish' the whisky in a different type of cask. The funnel used by Bruichladdich looks as old as the distillery.

Pages 8-9
Water supply
Lochindaal distillery, Port Charlotte, Islay

This is a particularly fascinating relic of the long closed Lochindaal Distillery at Port Charlotte on Islay. The buildings of Bruichladdich can be seen in the distance in the top left hand corner. All that remains of the old distillery are two particularly atmospheric warehouses used for storage by Bruichladdich, which now owns them. Plans are well advanced to bring the old distillery back to life and the appearance of a range of highly peated malts called PC4 - PC5 - PC6 (short for Port Charlotte) from Bruichladdich give us a foretaste of what to expect. It seemed fitting to compliment Jim McEwan's foreword with a view of his 'domain'.

Introduction

Pages 10-11
Barley floor – Stills – Excise office
Balvenie distillery, Dufftown – Springbank, Campbeltown – Knockdhu distillery, Huntly

Balvenie was my first distillery visit for photographic purposes more than five years ago, at which time this project was only beginning to formulate in my mind. Knockdhu is where it really took off and where, thanks to Malcolm Waring (now the manager of Pulteney in Wick), I carried out my first interviews. Springbank in Campbeltown holds a special place in my affections for its respect for historical tradition and for its unselfconscious beauty.

Pages 12-13
Warehouse – The yard
Glenfarclas, Speyside – Springbank distillery, Campbeltown

It is easy to forget that Campbeltown at the very foot of the Mull of Kintyre peninsular was, in Alfred Barnards' time, the heart of Scottish Malt distilling with 21 working distilleries. Now only Springbank, its new sibling Glengyle, and Glenscotia ,keep the tradition going. The atmospheric yard with its hilly backdrop is quite concealed from public view. The distillery, like the town, is insulated from rapid change, and is still run as a family business as is the beautiful Glenfarclas pictured opposite.

Raw materials peat – barley – water

Pages 16-17
The view from Highland Park peat bog
Hobbister hill, Orkney

Highland Park in Orkney is one of the few distilleries still using its own floor maltings. The peat is obtained from Hobbister Hill, near Kirkwall, where it is dug out from the peat beds and left to dry in an open slatted shed for several months before being used in the kiln. My romantic expectation that I would find an old man with a spade was rapidly disillusioned by a large yellow JCB operated by two Geordies. The view, however, was spectacular, and the presence of two red-throated divers on a nearby lochan added considerably to the mystique of the place.

Pages 20-21
Kiln peat supply
Bowmore distillery, Islay
Quote: retired stillman, Islay

I got up early in the morning at Bowmore in Islay to watch the kiln being lit. It was a remarkably similar process to lighting a domestic fire, even down to the use of matches and kindling. Like several other distilleries, Bowmore malts a percentage of its own barley, which is then combined with malt from other sources. Whether or not this is with an eye to tourism, it has an indefinable but powerful impact on the feel of the place and particularly on its smell. The slowly germinating barley has an earthy rustic aroma, which acts as a powerful reminder of the agricultural origins of the product.

Pages 24-25
Cooling water
Coleburn distillery, Rothes
Quote: retired distillery manager, Aberdeenshire

The beautiful buildings of Colemore distillery lie deep in the valley bottom between Elgin and Rothes. Regrettably, they are now completely empty of equipment and are awaiting conversion into an entertainment complex. On a beautiful morning with the frost on the roofs of the warehouses and the burn which provided the cooling water running down the side of the main buildings, it presented a peaceful scene, but one most unlikely to ever witness any more whisky production.

Pages 18-19
The drying out of cut peat
Hobbister hill, Orkney
Quote: retired stillman, Islay

Although nowadays we tend to associate the smoky peaty malts with the islands, my memory stretches back to my first taste of Glengarioch in the 1970s, when it had a very peaty character. Ardmore, which is fairly rarely found as a single malt, has retained its peaty quality, as has Benriach under its new owners and the experienced ministrations of Billy Walker. I was reliably informed that the peat quality in Islay and that on the east coast is quite different, and that an experienced blender would easily be able to distinguish between them.

Pages 22-23
The barley loft
Bruichladdich distillery, Islay
Quote: retired distillery manager, Speyside

The barley loft at Bruichladdich is enormous. Scattered throughout are relics of its past use, like the rakes and the screws for transporting the grain through the distillery. Nowadays, most of the barley goes to large commercial maltsters on the east coast, who malt to a very precise recipe given to them by the purchasing distillery. Only at Balvenie in Dufftown have I seen large heaps of barley prior to steeping, as must have once been the case in this highly atmospheric location.

Pages 26-27
Cooling tank
Talisker distillery, Isle of Skye
Quote: Manager (who might wish to remain anonymous!) But NOT from Talisker

High above the still house at Talisker, in what is probably one of the most beautiful locations for a distillery in Scotland, lies this rather remarkable cooling system, with the mirror-still surface of a water tank broken only by the vortex of the cooling pipe. The distillery itself lies only a few yards from the edge of the loch, with a smell of seaweed and brine ever-present. Somehow, by means unknown, those aromas end up in the whisky and have contributed to making it so justifiably famous.

Raw materials energy – casks – chemistry

Pages 28-29
Disused steam engine
Ardmore distillery, Kennethmont, Aberdeenshire
Quote: retired engineer, Kennethmont, Speyside

One of the unexpected pleasures of this project has been the discovery of pieces of obsolete equipment, often of quite stunning beauty, but in a very unselfconscious way which is hidden from tourists. This magnificent steam engine at Ardmore in Kennethmont is a good example, beautifully maintained by Gordon Grant. There is another one at Dalmore and a third at Longmorn in Elgin. Traces of water wheels can be found in a number of places most particularly at Dalmore and Strathisla. It is perhaps one of whiskies' strengths that it does not linger in the past but invests heavily in new technology wherever possible. Regrettably, the new equipment is rarely as photogenic as the old!

Pages 32-33
Auxillary generator
Bruichladdich distillery, Islay
Quote: retired manager, Aberdeenshire

This extraordinary piece of industrial history was the auxiliary generator at Bruichladdich until it was removed two years ago to make way for a more modern replacement. It brought back to me the world of steam railways, grease and hard graft which reflected the time when it was in general use. I believe it has now gone to a good home in a museum. The distillery in which it was housed is the very antithesis of the throwaway culture. However, there is no room for sentiment when a machine reaches the end of its useful life.

Pages 36-37
Belt drives
Glentauchers distillery, Keith
Quote: retired manager, Aberdeenshire

The drum maltings at Glentauchers are the most unusual unexpected feature of my entire project. I was introduced to them by Darren Hosie from Chivas, who obtained the enormous Victorian key from the still house. Housed in a small separate building connected by a walkway is a remarkable time capsule with all its machinery and belts in an intact state. Save for the activities of the ubiquitous pigeons, it offers a remarkable window into a lost world. Health and safety as we know it now did not even exist. Dangerous belts ran in every direction moving at high speed controlling the mills and the malting process. Only at Speyburn is there an equally beautiful but much better known set of Drum maltings. The picture on page 61 illustrates the main drum.

Pages 30-31
Bird's nest on power inlet (disused)
Dalmore distillery, Alness
Quote: retired engineer, Kennethmont, Speyside

Dalmore is one of my favourite distilleries, and also one of my favourite malts. I was introduced to its rather hidden delights by the late Drew Sinclair, who had spent his whole career in the same distillery, progressing up the ladder from warehouse man, where he started when he was 15. Underneath the shiny, glossy, tourist-friendly distillery there are layers like archaeological strata, reflecting practice in a former age. It was in one of these that I discovered this unusual location for a bird's nest, on top of the power input which is no longer used. To me it was like a metaphor for a place more in harmony with nature than most, sitting on the edge of the Dornoch Firth exposed to the gales and any passing sea life.

Pages 34-35
The stables
Brora distillery, Brora, Sutherland
Quote: retired cooper, Speyside

It took me a long time to get access to the iconic Brora distillery. The discovery of the distillery stables in an intact condition was the high point of the visit for me. Although there have been no horses in use for 50 years, one might have thought that the animals had moved out last week. I was told of a time when the stables flooded and the pigs, which were temporally housed there, were rescued from the attic into which they had floated or swum! I used the rather ingenious steps cut as semi-circular holes in the wood-panelled walls, which allowed me to inspect the scene of the crime. Pigeons are now the only inhabitants of the attic space.

Pages 38-39
Mill house
Dalmore distillery, Alness
Quote: retired manager, Speyside

The darkest and most subterranean part of Dalmore distillery is the Old Mill House, which used to provide the main power for the distillery. Unfortunately, the mill wheel is long gone but as you can see the Mill House is quite intact and contains the shafts and visible scoring on the walls made by the turning of the wheel. So old is this building that the ceiling is covered with small limestone stalactites. Drew Sinclair also showed me the remnants of an old steam engine at the same level in the distillery. The tourists enjoying the sparkling new visitors' centre never get to see this relic of the industrial past.

Pages 40-41
Casks after the rain
Ardbeg distillery, Islay
Quote: retired distillery manager, Speyside

I parked my motor home in a lay-by a few hundred yards from Ardbeg distillery and spent a night rocked by the Atlantic gales. In the morning the sun was out and the sky reflected beautifully from the water trapped on the surface of the barrels outside the distillery. Ardbeg lies at the end of a single-track road along the rocky South Shore of Islay beyond Laphroaig and Lagavulin. There is a feeling of being at the end of the road in every sense, in a wild and beautiful location totally exposed to the sea. The malt it produces is similarly extreme, much-fêted and loved by those who know, for its combination of smoke, seaweed and peat.

Pages 44-45
The yard
Pulteney distillery, Wick
Quote: retired stillman, Islay

This is a view of the yard at Pulteney distillery in Wick, Caithness. Pulteney is unusual these days for its city-centre location, surrounded by houses on all sides. The distillery is functional rather than beautiful, but it has a rather strong and distinct identity as an integral part of this very isolated town. The profile of the malt has been raised successfully by some inspiring and creative packaging, built around a very distinguished product.

Pages 48-49
Steeping tank
Mortlach distillery, Dufftown

This is either curious or disgusting, depending on your perspective. It's been several decades since these concrete steeping troughs were in use at Mortlach. Accumulated rainwater has led to a growth of brilliant orange moulds and algae. The old malt floors next door are intact as is the kiln, which still has its perforated floor to allow the germinated barley to dry in the hot air current. This was the only distillery in Dufftown to continue distilling during the war.

Pages 42-43
Abandoned cooperage
Ardmore distillery, Kennethmont
Quote: retired cooper, Speyside

Another favourite location is the abandoned cooperage at Ardmore distillery. This under-appreciated malt, with its peaty quality, has for long time been a significant component in Teacher's Highland cream. It's only very recently, under new ownership, that a distillery bottling of the single malt has become available. The cooperage has that 'Marie Celeste' quality that I particularly love. Items are just strewn about, much as they were left when casks were made here on a daily basis. The stencil for Teachers is visible in the picture.

Pages 46-47
Chemist's cupboard
Bladnoch distillery, Wigtown
Quote: retired manager, Islay

The chemists' cupboard at Bladnoch distillery has been very little changed since it was in regular use. The story of how this isolated but much respected distillery was rescued by Irish entrepreneur Raymond Armstrong – who couldn't bear the idea of owning a distillery without making whisky – is fascinating. He bought the premises as accommodation for holiday homes for Ulster policemen, but realised shortly afterwards that his mission was to resurrect the derelict distillery which had been known for a distinctive malt. The distillery is quirky and old-fashioned, but delightfully idiosyncratic. Some of the equipment seems held together largely through good will. Bladnoch will always be in short supply, but is a lovely malt prized by collectors.

Pages 50-51
Steeping tank
Balblair distillery, Edderton
Quote: retired mashman, Speyside

This is a view of the concrete steeping tank at Balblair distillery, Edderton, north of Inverness. During my visit I was told that a stopcock in the main distillery had fractured and a decision had been made to use one of the wheels in the picture as a replacement. Nobody had, however, anticipated that despite 40 years of disuse the plumbing was still connected, and the resulting jet of water took everybody by surprise and led to some very red faces. Balblair is a treasure house of interesting old equipment. Its malt deserves to be better known.

Germination   malt floor – drum malting – saladin malting

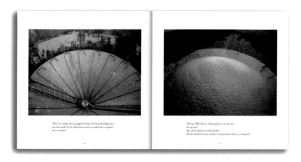

Pages 52-53
Steeping tanks in and out of use
Imperial distillery, Carron – Bowmore, Islay
Quote: retired distillery manager, Speyside

Imperial, at Carron, close to Aberlour, is probably the least picturesque of all the distilleries I have photographed. The scale of the machinery is enormous and 20 years of disuse give the place a forlorn, almost sinister atmosphere. The steeps are made of metal with a conical structure. Almost identical ones are still in active use at Bowmore, on Islay.

Pages 56-57
Malt floor rake
Bruichladdich distillery, Islay
Quote: retired distillery manager, Aberdeenshire

Looking after a floor malting is incredibly hard work. Glengarioch tried to bring it back in 2000, but the process was so labour-intensive that it only lasted a few months. Turning over the whole floor twice a day to ensure adequate aeration is an essential part of the process. This used to be done with rakes and spades but there are now mechanised spades to reduce the backbreaking effort. I found this rake in the barley store at Bruichladdich.

Pages 60-61
Drum maltings
Glentauchers distillery, Keith
Quote: retired manager, Speyside

This wonderful piece of Victorian engineering is a single drum malting at Glentauchers, near Keith. The drum was one device which mechanised the malting process by slowly turning its contents like an enormous washing machine until the barley began to germinate. The drum had an enormous door on one side, which could open when the barley was ready, depositing its contents on to a conveyor belt from where they would be taken to the kiln and later to the mill. This drum has lain disused for 35 years since the big commercial maltsters centralised the malting process for many different distilleries.

Pages 54-55
Malting floor
Bowmore distillery, Islay

Perhaps I am an old romantic, but the sight and aroma of a fully functioning floor malting gives an extra dimension to the atmosphere of a distillery. Highland Park, Springbank, Bowmore, Laphroig and Balvenie are the only ones still in active use. Tamdhu has a functioning Saladin maltings. There have been rumours that Benriach, now also the owner of Glendronach, might start to malt again. I find it difficult to believe that commercial maltsters can produce an identical product – although that is probably an irrational, unscientific view. The process is very labour-intensive and therefore not likely to find favour with accountants, as Glengarioch discovered to its cost in 2000.

Pages 58-59
Glory hole
Lagavulin distillery, Islay
Quote: retired mash man, Wick

This old blue barrow, long displaced by mechanisation, was in a storage shed at Lagavulin. The barley was taken from the steeps by a conveyor belt of small buckets and dropped onto the floor of the malting through a chute. The barrow would be held under the chute, filled and then taken to be distributed in a thick layer over the floor. It is worth asking why so many obsolete pieces of equipment are easy to find in the average distillery. I think a mixture of nostalgia and inertia is probably responsible. Sometimes in the case of the most complex pieces of machinery, it was cheaper just to leave them in place rather than attempt to dismantle them.

Pages 62-63
Saladin maltings
Benrinnes distillery, Aberlour
Quote: retired regional manager, Elgin

The most extreme solution to the labour-intensive nature of the malt floors was the development of the Saladin malting, an example of which you see in this picture. This one lies at Benrinnes, in the lee of the mountain of the same name, up the valley from Aberlour. The scale of it is enormous. The vaulted ceiling, which is reminiscent of church architecture, would probably have been demolished had it not been subject to a preservation order. The barley was pushed along huge concrete troughs by a large blue tractor resembling a snowplough, rolling along rails from one end of the malting to the other. This would allow enormous quantities of barley to be handled by only one man. Tamdhu is the only distillery which maintains a Saladin malting, but on a much reduced scale compared with that at Benrinnes.

Kilning

Milling

Pages 64-65
The malt floor
Glenglassaugh distillery, Portsoy
Quote: retired distillery manager, Speyside

This atmospheric shot of the old maltings at Glenglassaugh, near Portsoy, was taken through the grime-encrusted windows on account of a health and safety warning posted on the doors by a previous owner. This distillery is now being resurrected under the ownership of a Dutch investment group. It is known for a distinctive, honeyish malt, which has become increasingly difficult to find. At the time of taking this picture only the warehouses were in use, and that for storing casks from other distilleries.

Pages 68-69
The kiln
Highland Park distillery, Kirkwall, Orkney
Quote: retired manager, Islay

One of the few working distillery kilns in Scotland is to be found at Highland Park in Orkney. Local peat from Hobbister Hill is mixed with coal, and the kiln is stoked by hand with an ordinary spade. On the blackboard are written details of the kilning process. The barley is dried until its water content falls to about four per cent.

Pages 72-73
Inside the kiln during operation
Highland Park distillery, Kirkwall, Orkney
Quote: retired mash man, Wick

Watching the men operating in this environment was quite an eye-opener. They were dressed head-to-foot in rubber suits and wore helmets rather like deep-sea divers. All this was necessary to protect them from the dust as they shovelled the barley towards the chutes and screws which carry it towards the mill. It was difficult to imagine how awful it must have been to have to do this process without protection, as was the case in the past.

Pages 66-67
Malt screws
Tamdhu distillery, Speyside

Tamdhu was a great surprise to me. Totally without fanfare, it has a unique, functioning Saladin maltings. Huge steel troughs are filled with steeped barley, through which a series of revolving circular blades slowly move, turning over the barley as they pass by. When the barley germinates, screws like this one move the barley to the kiln. Tamdhu malts a lot more barley than it can use itself, so also supplies malt to other distilleries in the Edrington group, like Macallan and Highland Park.

Pages 70-71
Inside the kiln
Highland Park, Kirkwall, Orkney
Quote: retired mash man, Speyside

Trying to take pictures inside an operating kiln is akin to wandering in the jungle in Malaysia. The humidity levels are quite overwhelming, and only the most hardy of cameras can survive in such an environment – particularly when reliant on sophisticated electronics. My biggest problem was keeping the lens free of moisture. At Tamdhu they provided an initiation by allowing me to enter the oven immediately before the kiln. This was like being stuck in the Sahara Desert. I acquired a new empathy with the men who had related to me their tales of how it had been when the kiln had to be stripped out by hand.

Pages 74-75
Barley attic
Glentauchers distillery, Keith

This is a view of the barley dresser (a device to sift out stones and impurities from the grain) in the old abandoned maltings at Glentauchers. The drum on page 61 was part of this system, which is all belt driven and arranged so the grain can be stored germinated and milled all in one place before making its way into the mash tun in the main distillery. The picture is a high dynamic range image, which allows the contrast range to be adequately managed.

Milling   Mashing

Pages 76-77
Bucket-weighing machine
Bruichladdich distillery, Islay
Quote: retired manager, Aberdeenshire

This is a traditional example of a bucket-weighing machine, which catches the barley as it falls from the mill, allowing an exact record be kept of the weight of barley used for each mash. There is something fascinating about watching this river of grain until just enough has accumulated to trigger the mechanism which tips the bucket and discharges the contents. This particular mill has been in use at Bruichladdich for 100 years and requires very little maintenance.

Pages 80-81
Open-top mash tun
Bruichladdich distillery, Islay

The open mash tun at Bruichladdich is, as far as I know, unique. Watching the hot water and malted barley mix dropping into the tun through enormous brass spouts is like presiding over a huge vat of porridge. So much steam is produced that the mashman can only just be discerned at the controls from the other side of the tun. The water comes in at 140°F. The stirring gear starts to rotate and bits emerge from the broth looking for all the world like a miniature Loch Ness monster!

Pages 84-85
Stirring gear, mash tun
Springbank distillery, Campbeltown
Quote: retired manager, Speyside

The stirring gear in the mash tun has to be taken apart from time to time for cleaning. At the bottom of the tun a large number of metal plates with perforations fit together to allow the sugary wort to be drained off at the end of the mash. Usually, the mashes are sequential, with traces of the last mash still present as the new input of malted barley and hot water fills the container. This is an example of tun equipment from Springbank. More modern distilleries are equipped with stainless-steel stirrers and automatic emptying, which makes cleaning much more simple.

Pages 78-79
Dressing machine
Springbank distillery, Campbeltown
Quote: retired mash man, Speyside

Beside the barley loft at Springbank, in Campbeltown, is this example of an old Victorian dressing machine which prepares the barley prior to milling. Springbank is a wonderfully atmospheric distillery. Large parts of it have remained almost unaffected by the changes wrought on most distilleries over the last 30 years by processes of automation. This gives it the quality of a living, working museum. Unprotected belts carrying malted barley and copious dust traverse the barley loft next to this mill.

Pages 82-83
Pot ale containers
Bladnoch distillery, Wigtown
Quote: retired manager, Speyside

The disposal of waste products is a big problem for distilleries. In Islay, all the distilleries truck their waste across the island to a point above the straits of Jura, where the currents in the channel between the islands run fast enough to allow safe discharge through an underground pipe. The solution at Bladnoch pictured here is rather more simple. The pot ale is accumulated in these large rusty tanks and is eventually run onto the surrounding agricultural land by agreement with the farmers.

Pages 86-87
Mash tun controls
Bruichladdich distillery, Islay
Quote: retired cooper, Aberdeenshire

The controls above the mash tun at Bruichladdich are simple but necessary. Getting up at six in the morning to watch the first mash of the day is a memorable event. Steam is everywhere as the tun has no lid. There is an interesting very British compromise at play here as the temperature of the water which enters the tun is taken in Fahrenheit whereas after going through the cooler then entering the wash backs it enters the world of centigrade!

Fermentation

First distillation

Pages 88-89
Mash tun controls
Strathisla distillery, Keith
Quote: retired stillman, Aberdeenshire

This wonderful, gleaming piece of brassware comes from one the oldest distilleries in Scotland, at Strathisla in Keith. Unlike many of the oldest distilleries, equipment here is maintained in immaculate condition despite its age. The whole distillery has a very intimate feel, with small stills and metal walkways connecting different parts of the process. At the rear lie the regional headquarters of the Chivas group now owned by Pernod Ricard of France.

Pages 92-93
Washbacks
Old Macallan distillery, Rothes
Quote: retired stillman, Islay

Macallan is an immaculately clean, highly automated distillery, with a deservedly high reputation. Lying behind the main still house is an unobtrusive building containing the original distillery, which has been mothballed since 1980. It is now being brought back into service as a result of increased demand. This old distillery has been largely left alone but sufficient care has been taken to ensure that the washbacks were kept filled with water in a state of potential readiness for future use. In view of the recent announcement regarding its refurbishment this would seem to have been a very wise move.

Pages 96-97
Water top-up tank
Balmenach distillery, Cromdale
Quote: retired mashman, Speyside

This water top-up tank at Balmenach, in Cromdale, lies at the edge of the old engine house which, despite being surplus to requirements, has an amazing patina of age and use. Balmenach lies high up on the mountainside in a situation which must have been wild and inaccessible during the deep snowfalls of the past. It has an enormous disused Saladin maltings and great potential to have a higher profile than in recent years.

Pages 90-91
Washbacks
Old Macallan distillery, Rothes

This is a stunning set of washbacks, out of use since 1980, but now being refurbished. Before the era of automation the washbacks were cleaned with besoms (a broom made from heather tied onto a sturdy staff). Caustic was used to sterilise the wood and it was then well flushed with water. Now high pressure steam has replaced both and is a good deal less dangerous. The natural bacterial culture of the wood was believed to play a significant role in the fermentation. Many distillers swear by wooden washbacks but others seem quite happy with stainless steel. Macallan has both.

Pages 94-95
Stills
Pulteney distillery Wick

These 'bathyscaphes' are reminiscent of Jacques Cousteau's diving bells. The window on the still is a visual aid for the stillman to ensure that the still doesn't 'boil over' with undistilled wort, frothing over into the cooling arm. These days heating by steam coils makes control relatively easy. In the past, when stills were heated directly by coal fires, control was very difficult; rather like cooking in a coal fired Aga or Rayburn. If the fermentation hadn't quite finished soap was added to prevent excess frothing (strange but true!).

Pages 98-99
Coal ovens
Glendronach distillery, Forgue, Aberdeenshire
Quote: retired warehouseman, Aberdeenshire

This picture dates from 2002 and is the oldest in this collection. Glendronach, near Forgue Huntly in Aberdeenshire, has always been one of my favourites. I first visited it in the late 1970s and remember the wonderfully atmospheric floor maltings. The picture shows the coal-fired stills, which were the last in Scotland and have now been replaced by gas, which is more easily automated. The control of coal-fired stills required considerable skill in order to avoid the still boiling over or burning its contents.

Second distillation

Pages 100-101
Still controls
Old Macallan distillery, Rothes
Quote: retired coppersmith, Dufftown

Another picture of the remarkable old Macallan distillery, which is now being refurbished. It has been my ambition in this project to record things as they actually are, rather than to clean them up for the sake of aesthetic considerations. This has meant that some distilleries are just too clean for my purposes. I did not just want to replicate the many books on distilleries full of gleaming polished brass and immaculate stainless steel. That explains why, in a picture such as this one, I have not removed the piece of rubbish because in my view it adds to the picture.

Pages 104-105
Spirit safe
Springbank distillery, Campbeltown
Quote: retired excise officer, Wisbech, Cambs

This picture, to me, encapsulates the mysterious atmosphere of Springbank distillery, with its reverence for the past and its disdain for cosmetics. The spirit safe, which is at the very heart of production, is literally held together with pieces of wire. Everything in the place has been tried and tested for generations and something about that unselfconscious authenticity finds its way into the wonderful malt whisky which it produces.

Pages 108-109
Spirit safe
Jura distillery, Jura
Quote: retired mash man, Wick

The verdigris inside the spirit safe of Jura distillery makes an unusual and colourful picture. This idiosyncratic distillery has spent a large part of its life out of operation but was completely rebuilt in the 1960s and lies on one of the most beautiful islands off the south Scottish coast, accessible only by ferry from Islay. The unpeated nature of the spirit also sets it apart from the Islay distilleries. Regrettably there is little trace of its lengthy history prior to a disastrous fire in the 1920s.

Pages 102-103
Disused spirit safe
Benriach distillery, Elgin

Benriach has been reborn and has the potential to be one of the most complete sites in eastern Scotland. Its floor maltings were only discontinued a few years ago and could easily be restarted. This old disused spirit safe caught my eye for the vivid layer of corrosion and verdigris. Above the maltings are a splendid barley store, dresser and mill, all in a glowing wood veneer. The malts, which Billy Walker is producing from old stock, remind me of the long abandoned east coast smoky character. When the new malts come on stream in a few years time I suspect they will be worth waiting for.

Pages 106-107
Still house
Rosebank distillery, Falkirk
Quote: retired stillman, Aberdeenshire

Gaining access to Rosebank distillery turned out to be rather comical. Over the last few years it has been owned by the water board, lying as it does on the banks of the Forth Clyde Canal. When the day came to take pictures the key proved stubbornly reluctant to work and we ended up having to break in by shinning over a high wall. Much of the content, including the stills, was surprisingly intact, despite 20 years of dereliction. Uncertainty still surrounds the future of this iconic distillery, but I think it has passed the point where its resurrection is even a possibility.

Pages 110-111
Spirit safe
Glen Scotia, Campbeltown
Quote: retired stillman, Islay

This colourful spirit safe belongs to probably the strangest distillery I have visited: Glen Scotia in Campbeltown. From the outside, the buildings look derelict and, with a workforce of only three using extremely antiquated equipment, the single malt continues to be produced sometimes by borrowing staff from the nearby Springbank distillery, which has a completely separate ownership. Other than the safe, the bright blue metal washbacks made an extraordinary sight. The presence of this distillery adds to the variety of Scottish distilling, and I would be loath to see it disappear.

Maturation excise – warehousing – racking

Pages 112-113
Derelict warehouse
Glenglassaugh distillery, Portsoy

Glenglassaugh has several modern racked warehouses but also two derelict dunnage warehouses, of which this is one. Stock was removed in the nick of time before the roof came in. Restoration of these beautiful buildings is on the agenda for the future but will have to take its place in the queue behind more essential work required to help the distillery reclaim its reputation, described by Alfred Barnard, in 1887, as, 'too well known to need any praise here'.

Pages 116-117
Excise officers' rooms
Bunnahabhain and Laphroig, Islay
Quote: retired mash man, Speyside

The excise officer's room in the warehouse at Bunnahabhain looks more like an interrogation cell from a former Soviet prison. Frequently, the offices contain books, dossiers and memos covered with a thick layer of dust and not consulted for 30 or more years. Sometimes they are converted for other purposes, as at Springbank and Bruichladdich, where they are used to sample specimens from the warehouse.

Pages 120-121
Warehouse
Glenlivet, Speyside
Quote: retired excise officer, Wisbech, Cambs

The warehouses at Glenlivet are particularly impressive. This picture comes from the upper floor of a two-floor warehouse. I was struck by the unusual windows and venting, which just throw enough natural light on the contents to create a mysterious scene. This beautiful distillery lies at the head of a lovely valley. It has an appealing disused cooperage and some really ancient warehouses, but otherwise is a very modern, highly-automated distillery.

Pages 114-115
Excise office
Glenglassaugh distillery, Portsoy
Quote: retired cooper, Speyside

In the corner of a disused warehouse at Glenglassaugh lies this amazingly atmospheric excise officers' room. Until the centralisation of excise services in 1975, each distillery had a resident officer who held the keys to the warehouses and kept extensive records for his bosses in Edinburgh and London. The relationship between the officer and the distillery manager was often a very close one, and the officer was sometimes accused of "going native" because his role as an unofficial policemen frequently put him in conflict with the workforce.

Pages 118-119
Warehouses
Bladnoch distillery, Wigtown
Quote: retired manager, Speyside

The warehouses at Bladnoch look like a film set from Whisky Galore. Scattered throughout are sampling glasses left as in the aftermath of a party, but probably reflecting some sampling earlier that day. Bladnoch is still forced to rely on the remains of supplies from its past, but in the very near future the results of Raymond Armstrong's energy and efforts should appear on the market.

Pages 122-123
Racking
Bruichladdich distillery, Islay
Quote: retired cooper, Aberdeenshire

During its long years of maturation in the warehouses, malt whisky can remain in the same barrel for its entire life, or more commonly these days be transferred for a short time into a different cask to impart a specific flavour to the finished product. This process is known as racking and, at Bruichladdich, makes use of an amazingly ancient filter funnel – pictured here – to transfer the contents from one barrel to another.

Bruichladdich malt screws

ACKNOWLEDGMENTS

Interviewees

The following kindly agreed to be interviewed and recorded. Transcribed pieces of those interviews appear on most pages. The dates of their working life in distilleries are shown in brackets, if known.

Denzil Chesters – retired exciseman, Auchentoshan distillery (1968-1976)

John Connon – retired manager, Speyburn Mortlach and Glengarioch distilleries
(1938-1982)

Bill Craig – retired regional manager, Hiram Walker (1965-1995)

Neil Ferguson – retired stillman, Caol Ila (1969-2000)

Gordon Grant – retired engineer, Ardmore distillery (1956-93)

Sandy Grant – retired coppersmith, Grants of Dufftown (1934-1984)

Calcoat Harper – retired manager, Glencadam and regional manager, Allied distilleries (1965-1995)

Frank Massie – retired manager, Glendronach and Ardmore (1972-2004)

Bill Mclean – retired cooper and former baker, Knockdhu distillery (1960-1995)

Rhuari McLeod – retired Assistant manager, Bruichladdich and Jura distilleries (1950-1985)

Beall McWilliam – warehouseman and Mason Imperial, Glentauchers, Knockdhu (1960-2007)

Ronnie Mennie – retired manager, Glendronach and Ardmore (1967-1996)

John Munro – retired stillman and former lorry driver, Glenfarclas distillery (1970-2004)

Drew Sinclair – late manager, Dalmore distillery (1957-2006)

'Beakie' Sutherland – retired stillman, Brora

Alistair (Tosh) Wares – retired stillman, Pulteney distillery (1969-1995)

Ian Whitely – retired exciseman, Glentauchers, Knocdhu

I cannot thank these men enough for their humour, generosity of spirit and kindness.
I have protected their anonymity by not attributing specific quotes to an individual.
The following people have given me invaluable assistance over the last five years:

Special thanks

Dr Euan Thompson, who made the initial introductions to Inver House for me.

Malcolm Waring, then at Knockdhu, now at Pulteney, for launching my interviews with panache.

Peter Currie and Mark Reynier, of Springbank and Bruichladdich respectively, for having the confidence to invite me to take more pictures for use by their companies.

Darren Hosie of Chivas, for his patience and encouragement.

Stuart Nickerson of Glenglassaugh, who gave me permission to use images taken for the company as a commission.

My friend Clare Peters and also Carol Robson who helped me with the transcribing.

also

Fred Sinclair – Manager, Pulteney
Derek Sinclair – Manager, Balblair
Dennis Malcolm – Manager, Balmenach
Alistair Longwell – Manager, Ardmore
Jockie Paterson – Manager, Glentauchers/Imperial
Kenny Grant – Acting manager, Glengarioch
Bobby Anderson – Manager, Speyburn
Doug Fitchett – Manager, Glencadam
David Doig – Manager, Fettercairn
Raymond Armstrong – Manager/owner, Bladnoch
Stuart Thompson – Manager, Ardbeg
Ishbel Mactaggart – Operations manager, Bowmore
Billy Stitchell – Manager, Caol Ila
Billy Johnston – Operator, Laphroig
John Campbell – Chief brewer, Laphroig
Peter Smith – Operations executive, Diageo
Lorraine Martin – Human resources, Diageo
John Thompson – Manager, Lagavulin

John McLellan – Manager, Bunnahabhain
Michael Heads – Manager, Jura
Willy Cochrane – Head brewer, Jura
Scott Bitters – Operations manager, Benrinnes
Heather Anderson – Public relations, Tamdhu
Ian Chalmers – Public relations, Tamdhu
Scott Jordan – Brewer, Oban
Kenny Gray – Manager, Oban
Charlie Smith – Manager, Talisker
Vicky McKaskill – Talisker
Colin Ross – Manager, Ben Nevis
John Carmichael – Manager of visitor centre, Ben Nevis
Billy Walker – Manager, Benriach
Yvonne Thackeray – Public relations, Chivas Keith
Alistair Brown – Manager, Tobermory
Mark Lochhead – Manager, Clynelish/Brora
Ian McWilliam – Operations manager, Glenfarclas

The above roles were, as far as I can check, those held at the time of assistance, but rates of turnover in the industry make it likely that many of these people have moved on.
I apologise if I have incorrectly described anyone's role in the company or omitted anyone by accident.

A note on the photography

All pictures were taken on digital equipment. Initially I used a Hasselblad H1 with
an Imacon 128C back, which produced 21Mp files. This has been replaced by
a Hasselblad H3D, which produces 39Mp files, each of which occupies 200Mb.
Storage is a problem!

These cameras were occasionally augmented by a Nikon D2X, recently updated to
a Nikon D3. The vast majority was taken in natural light. Very little post processing
has been necessary. There are a few examples of high dynamic range processing,
whereby several photographs at different exposures are combined together by
Photomatix software. This transcends the technical problems inherent in dark,
high-contrast locations. Both cameras performed faultlessly, even in the most
demanding of conditions.

First published 2009 by Envisage Books

Copyright © 2009 by Ian Macilwain

A catalogue record for this book is available from the British Library.

ISBN 978 0 9541011 6 9

Design and production by Eddie Ephraums
Envisage Books
www.envisagebooks.com

Printed by C&C Offset Printing Co., Ltd., China